Taher Adel is a British-Bahraini p
has an MA in Creative Writing a
East Anglia in 2021. He was p
the-sea in 2019. His poems h
SMOKE Magazine, The New Eu
Magazine, Tedx, Poetry London Magazine and Poetry Salzburg
Review.

I don't know what language I dream in

Taher Adel

Burning Eye

BurningEyeBooks
**Never Knowingly
Mainstream**

This edition published by Burning Eye Books 2023

www.burningeye.co.uk

@burningeyebooks

Burning Eye Books
15 West Hill, Portishead, BS20 6LG

ISBN 978-1-913958-40-4

I don't know what language I dream in was first published by Ambit Magazine
Twelve Million was first published by Poetry London
Pilgrim was first published by UEA Anthology 2020
Mass was first published by Lucent Dreaming
Son was first published by Glassworks
Coiled was first published by Poetry Salzburg

Contents

I don't know what language I dream in

My mother speaks to me only in Arabic
because you'll learn English in school.
But when did I lose my mother tongue?
Was it when I first visited my homeland
and had to translate words back to English
or was it when I saw my mum crying to a eulogy
and felt nothing?
If your mother tongue is no more,
does that make your tongue an orphan?
Is that why I don't know what language I dream in?
Did you know Arabic has eleven words for *love*
and over one hundred words for *camel*
but no word for someone who has lost his mother tongue?

Twelve Million

The letter ح does not exist in any other language.
It's pronounced as *h*
but imagine your lungs are struggling for breath.
Is that why حب *hub* is the most common word for love,
because both leave you
gasping for air?

There are twelve million words in the Arabic language.
Therefore, an Arab can tell you exactly
how much he loves you in more ways
than there are words in the entire French dictionary,
but only one is seen as the language of love.

Friday Lepidoptera

They visit every Friday,
sometimes as *Maniola jurtina*
or, if they really miss us,
Zerynthia rumina.

They sit on our windowsills
or blend with the curtains
with eyes on their wings
and the only nectar they are after
is smiles and laughter.

Is that why Aristotle named them
after the soul?
Is that why my father would spring
open the windows to let them all in
so that we could wonder
what relative has visited us today?

Pilgrim

I carried my mother's pain and prayers
a thousand miles to a shrine found near the Euphrates.
They said this man gave up everything
and now the angels listen intently
to every broken heart that comes
begging   I carried her pain and prayers like
a fisherman showing the angels my tears,
hoping one would take the bait   I struggled to supplicate,
remembering half the words, but the sentiment remained.

But how do you know your prayers are answered?
One told me the key is to travel on your feet
without spilling your intentions   like hot chai in small cups,
walking from one city to the other, from one father to another
until your shoulders are rounded in worship
and your toes are stamped with heart-shaped blisters.
Only then would the heavens look towards your soul
and take the pain you carry.

So I thought of Zainab and carried on walking.

Suwayq

This town's symbol is a camel,
as the people here are known for their loyal relationship
with the desert transporter.
We have always been Bedouins –
no, that's untrue –
we are Adnanite settlers, descendants of Ishmael.
Our rightful home, I suppose,
would be between Safa and Marwa,
where Hajar ran her heels into the ground until water sprung.
Was the miracle the water or the lineage that trickled forth?

This close affinity to motherhood
might be the reason why this town is kind towards its camels,
or why there is a constellation
my forebears named *the Protecting Mother Camels.*
Maybe I'm overthinking.

My great-grandfather was supposedly a simple man,
but even simple men can be shaken awake by dreams,
explained only as morsels from the future.
He stumbled across bits and pieces of it,
fixated on a star like a sailor drunk on fate,
until it took him away from Suwayq,
and now here I am in Bedfordshire
writing about how a son can find meaning
in an old town symbol.

Beijerinck's Law

Everything is everywhere, but the environment selects.

Martinus Beijerinck

like fern spores we ride the earth's breath
settling even in the most uninhabitable places
the soil takes one look at us and lobs us out

we fly again

until the wintertime taunts us but we defrost
eventually bearing life that is pulled
from root for not being endemic enough

we fly again

until we camouflage with the native foliage
until our green is measured for assimilation
until they realise we are not green but brown

we fly again

until the winds no longer call our name
until the houses become our houses
and the soil becomes our soil
until *everything is everywhere*

Reading practice

'What does it say?'

the question that comes before
the worried eyes
the heavy breathing that follows
every word you read
wondering if these are the words
that encompass the power to free
or the ones that will wipe out dreams

all I know is that this shouldn't be
what a seven-year-old should see

the words as complicated as the
distress
on your father's face
made thicker because he too
cannot read

Asylum Rejected

'What does that mean?'

Hand-knotted Tribe

There are five common Arabic words
for family, but
for most Arabs a nuclear family
is not even a phrase worthy of conversation.
We raise our own like vertical threads
tied onto the loom
and grandfathers, grandmothers, uncles and aunts
make up the horizontal threads
that intertwine to create a foundation where
each knot is tied, cut and tied again;
this we call a tribe.

So when one knot finds itself untangled
and on a plane to unknown lands
it cannot make it back onto the rug;
that's why they call it cutting ties.
Sending photographs via airmail
will not patch things up, nor packing
Primark gifts in a suitcase to fill the years lost,
because this untangled knot
has become subsumed into a quilt,
so I guess FaceTime will do, for now.

Mass

The 1991 uprisings were a series of popular rebellions in Iraq between March and April 1991.

Even if nobody visits,
tombstones remain guarding the night like
coordinates in a constellation.
Once the earth spins enough
on its axis and the planets align
each star has its day to shine more brightly;
I'm not to be forgotten.
But what of those in unmarked graves?

Loved men lost in a sea of unknown limbs,
but where do we begin to sift
when bodies are found scattered
side by side, like a deck of cards laid out,
an abandoned magic trick,
distinguished by the shape of the bullets?
This lot here were killed in April by a Zastava M84,
skulls with identical bullet holes,
but none look like our king of hearts;
maybe he's in another gravesite?

Years later and we still polish your shoes
and leave them by the door.
Your remains were never found
so we remain waiting.
Maybe for our sake you'll return.
Your daughter is a woman now.
I'm sure you'll recognise her by her eyes;
they are exactly how you left them,
they are exactly yours.

Son

Don't forget
the ones you fail
to resurrect like
high books on
dusty shelves,
stories we open
for antique smells
but never to read again.

Don't forget the steps,
the ones they took for your peace.
Don't forget the way they would leave
their unwanted colour on doorsteps,
walking barefoot on streets.
Don't forget the loneliness –
shying away from conversation
because their words were beautiful
but would take too long to utter.

Don't forget the tongue
that is no longer a mother
because mothers die
and daughter tongues
cannot remember.

Don't forget the strength
it took to raise us tall
or the way they were
stripped of it all
piece by piece
until all that
remained was

you.

Coiled

Who you are is boiled down to two chains
coiled around each other, perfectly intimate and separate,
full of stories written in code, outliving bones
that are shelved under layers of earth,
so why do I feel lost?

Sometimes I feel my chains uncoil
and perform a chokehold around my mind
until I gasp from right to left
and for a sweet moment, every thought echoes in عربي .[1]

Sometimes my origins could not be more green
if I was pulled from the rugged trunk of a sycamore tree,
bones nourished by gold-top milk,
tongue baptised by the Thames
taught hopscotch by a blonde girl no older than ten.

Sometimes I beg for the sun to send a messenger
to resuscitate my dormant melanin and tell me
this too can be your home.

---

1   *Arabic*

م

m is said to be the first sound a baby can make
and that's why almost every language refers to mother
by this letter

and it often takes two months for them to learn
how to smile simply from observing the happiness
on your face
a seed sprouting from the corner of your heart
to the edges of their mouths

your womb no longer a home for them inside
instead it has taken the shape of your arms
and the comfort of your warmth
that's why the hardest thing for a mother
is to let go of her own
because the whole world is an extension
of her womb

I have fallen madly in love

I have fallen
madly in love
with your abjad,
with your alphabet,
with each and every
dotted mark, point and curve
that makes your body speak.
I wake up to your light
like the sun on the lap of ن
and bask in the glory of your ظ and ل
until my eyes are jaded in awe and و,
and then I sleep beneath your moon,
finding you camped between
م and ج, spoken in dreams
and in the ninety-nine names
beginning and ending with
بِسْمِ اللهِ الرَّحْمَنِ الرَّحِيمِ

You are full of consonants
because your vowels, like my sighs,
are lost between your markings,
and there are no capitals here,
just sounds, i'jam and harakat,
words turning you into poetry
and ink spinning itself into art,
for how beautiful must you be
to have your letters eternally
and faithfully
kissed by pens and stars?

سَلَام

a language spoken
beyond vibrations
the language of longing
the desire for the soul
to drop its chaos
to leave it by the door
so take a piece of me
take my peace
let us be where
two oceans meet
in calm
so show me your palms
let me be your shore
and you be mine

Twenty-Eight Letters

Arabic has twenty-eight letters in its alphabet,
fourteen belonging to the sun,
fourteen owned by the moon.

Sun letters are pronounced with
the front part of your tongue
like crowns of honour,
so when you introduce them
the ل is lost in their light
and forgotten,

but ل will always be pronounced
in words owned by the moon
because the moon will never say لا [2]
to love.

Constellations

You are the dots I connect
when I need a starry night,
forever changing but a pattern
I can rely on,
one, two, three and even Orion.

You have always been engraved on me
like the tablets of Mesopotamia,
the heavenly bodies of Ptolemy
built grand in my sky
like the twenty-eight mansions of China.

Greenhouse Diaspora

I open the door.
I take in the hot ghee-filled air,
leaving my naturalised tongue on the floor,
replacing it with my unkempt tongue from back home.
Salam, Mama.

There she is in her natural habitat,
humming away to religious anecdotes
like a bird whose nest is far from home,
yet she's singing all the right notes.
God does not burden any soul with
more than it can bear.

Sometimes I would hark back,
sideways tilting and wilting leaves
despite outgrowing my mother tree.
She now walks hunched and small
just so that my leaves can soak it all.

I leave again,
but the cold outside always brings me back home,
reminding me of where it truly is:
not in the desert oasis 4,000 miles away,
not the winter climate that shakes my roots today.
Home is not the mask I put on.
Home is not my mother tongue
but the vibrations of my mother's tongue.

Nails through wall

you take us in
ask us to spell our names
so that you can mispronounce them
until our names become over years
whatever you feel comfortable with
so long as the burgundy passport, now blue
protects us at borders you carved up
for vultures
you can call us whatever you please

you gave us what our country could never
a home
a chance to grow, albeit in shade
in corners littered with similar stories
we are grateful but anxious
invisible yellow stars branded
trying to build our future, your future
while avoiding your Medusa gaze
pirouetting away
as quickly as the colourful spinning tops
that make the front pages
of the *Daily Mail*

we always shy away
keeping to our colour, reminders of the past
people who share stories of whereabouts
near enough to the places of our birth
not quite Manama or Bangalore
but close enough when you tell us to go back home
we stay out of your way, a guest respecting
his host, we stitch your hearts back together
and we litter the wards
midwives snipping umbilical cords
guests sweeping more than dirty floors
but when self-made problems arrive at your door

you still hit us like nails through wall
until we are one with the bricks
covered in white paint and varnish
until there is nothing but this

The date-bearing phoenix

Phoenix dactylifera

my grandmother is a date tree
carrying us, clumped together
generations ripened by time
her eyes have seen too much
so cataract clouds try to dim her sun
and years cannot force her open hand
shut, her generosity remains a harvest

the years may have bent her back
but not her will
she stands as tall as any mother could
you cannot cut nor burn her down
she is a forever phoenix
that rises time and time again
from the ashes of her gadoo
and like a chimney
with smoke-hardened lungs
we all breathe her in
she is both the hearth and the heart
of our lineage, we cling on
like dates
refusing to let go
until we shrivel and fall
cut down by hooks
and distant travel
packaged in boxes
with exotic labels
but we still feel the
embrace of years
because she made sure that
we taste just like her

timeless

Pearl-diving colony

before oil there was a pearl boom
and this island country had divers
trained for centuries
in and out they would go
dolphins of the two seas
breaths held in and
hands open like shelled molluscs
manipulated slowly
by merchant monopoly
rendered redundant
products of aeons shoved aside
for cultured replicas
diving boats replaced with oil tankers
the smell of it enticed the arrival of
colonial flags in supposed aid
to quell and repel the Bedouins
Persians, Ottomans
tightening their chokehold
with one hand and drilling for oil
with the other
but it's ironic how when we left the land
of pearls and palms
to dive into crammed terraced houses
we were told to *go home*
a statement we were never brave
enough to say to them when they
arrived at our shores
or brave enough to say to ourselves
now

Muslim Boy

Boy waits until the dinner lady
puts fresh sponge cakes out for dessert;
it's time.
Boy finds a prayer mat.
'Where is Mecca?'
Exactly where it was yesterday,
just a few degrees past SE,
between the window and the radiator.
Boy has exactly six minutes until
he's caught again.

Boy holds his stomach
after scoring twice as many as his friends.
'You don't have to fast, you know?'
Boy still nutmegs his friends without thinking.
Boy still completes equations in record time.
The bell rings.
'Not even water?'
Not even water.
He has exactly four more hours to go
until samosas introduce Maghrib.

Man grows his beard because it masks
his double chin and complements his
complexion.
Brown people grow very luscious beards,
but not like the Scandinavians,
the handsome non-terrorist rugged look,
it's-safe-to-look-inside-my-rucksack look,
the non-is-he-practising-I've-seen-him-pray look.
He has exactly two more centimetres left
before he catches glares at work again.

Man waits until his colleagues have left.
It was time for Dhuhr three hours ago;
it's dark now, but better safe than sorry.

At least his assignments were handed in on time.
He wonders if prayer is like an assignment.
He wonders what it would be like to hear the call
to pray, to follow worshippers into mosques.
'I'll be out shortly, go ahead, I'll follow you.'
He has exactly ten minutes before
anybody pays attention.

These Seas

A reincarnated pearl diver
diving headfirst into ancestral seas,
finding pearls that resemble faces.
Each dive is one summer holiday,
two decades claimed until I have enough
for a necklace that proves I am from here,
no longer a tourist with virgin eyes
but one that has memorised
the graveyard and where to find
each ancestor, their bleary tombstones
rising in and out of centuries
like dolphins; these seas
are what makes us Bahrani.

These seas smell of fishing boats and
gadoo-stained fingers.
These seas sound like waves of
mosques blaring not far apart
and the clanking of coins
in my grandmother's purse,
enough to buy a whole family
smiles.

These seas feel like wrinkles
of old age, waves and waves,
for they have spent too
much time here, roots like veins
flowing into one another,
a seabed of love and pain.

These seas look like a painful utopia
and we look like longing birds.
We, the opera of the lost.

As Tall as Dad

My son's biggest fear in life right now
is that he won't be as tall as Dad
while I'm here trying to puzzle out
why inflation is rising and what the world
will look like when he finally becomes a man,
whether his Arabic will be just as broken,
whether the colour of his skin will remain
a problem,
whether he will find God all around him
yet pray in secret, whether he will soften
the ح of his name because the pronunciation
will expose his origins.
My son's biggest fear in life right now
is that he won't be as tall as Dad
and I hope it stays that way.

Sing back the lost notes

Today is one of those days where
I wish I could claw back time
and crawl back
into my ancestors' bodies,
walk where their feet have walked,
all robe and all sandal.
I want my home sun
to sing back the lost notes
found in my sleeping melanin.
I want to look up at a palm tree,
count the dates like an unopened
advent calendar.
I'm tired of all things Gregorian.
I want to surrender
my days to the moon
and know its phases just like it
memorises our changing faces.

I want to remove my tongue
like a wingless bird,
unclasping my native stutters.
I want to hatch a new one
in the nest of my ancestors.
I want to see old souls hurry
to the sound of prayer.
I want to hear minarets compete
with one another,
quaking birds of dawn.
I want to smell the sea upon waking
like a scented baptism,
a wash of the soul
drawing me close to the shore.
I want to climb into a boat like one
would climb out of a nightmare.

Arabic organ of love

At one point in time
the liver was the organ of love,
the vessel which stores
it all, a bittersweet hub.
Have you seen a liver before?
It's shaped like a capsized boat
that somehow still carries us all,
but unlike hearts
livers don't break;
they only scar and leak.
When they scar, they heal,
and when they leak, we float,
and even when they're cleaved
open, they grow again,
because livers are the only organs
that regenerate
so long as there is someone.

Who is your someone?

Quietly in my sleep

Was my mother tongue taken
quietly in my sleep
one random night,
or was it pulled from my gums,
a baby robin dragging
worms out of my mother's mouth,
or did it slowly wither away
each time I stepped outside into the cold
until sentences slowly froze, moon and sun letters
making way for the English *-ing*
instead of definitive Arabic endings,
placing celestial objects on finite strings
until bright meaning was lost,
becoming almost nothing?

How can all those lullabies
suddenly succumb to another language,
the cradle of my tongue's civilisation
colonised without even
giving me a choice,
a chance to say لا – *no?*

Milton Keynes UK
Ingram Content Group UK Ltd.
UKHW010838240823
427411UK00005B/113

9 781913 958404